JUPITER

Susan Ring

www.av2books.com

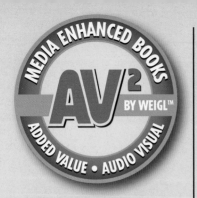

AV² provides enriched content that supplements and complements this book. Weigl's AV² books strive to create inspired learning and engage young minds in a total learning experience.

Your AV² Media Enhanced books come alive with...

Audio
Listen to sections of the book read aloud.

Key Words
Study vocabulary, and complete a matching word activity.

Video
Watch informative video clips.

Quizzes
Test your knowledge.

Go to **www.av2books.com**, and enter this book's unique code.

BOOK CODE

W 5 6 4 9 9 7

Embedded Weblinks
Gain additional information for research.

Slide Show
View images and captions, and prepare a presentation.

AV² by Weigl brings you media enhanced books that support active learning.

Try This!
Complete activities and hands-on experiments.

... and much, much more!

Published by AV² by Weigl
350 5th Avenue, 59th Floor
New York, NY 10118
Website: www.av2books.com   www.weigl.com

Library of Congress Cataloging-in-Publication Data

Ring, Susan.
Jupiter / Susan Ring.
    p. cm. -- (Our solar system)
Audience: 4-6.
Includes index.
ISBN 978-1-62127-264-9 (hardcover : alk. paper) -- ISBN 978-1-62127-273-1 (softcover : alk. paper)
1. Jupiter (Planet)--Juvenile literature. I. Title. II. Series: Our solar system (AV2 by Weigl)
QB661.R56 2014
523.45--dc23
                                2012044374

Printed in the United States of America in North Mankato, Minnesota
1 2 3 4 5 6 7 8 9 0 17 16 15 14 13

032013
WEP300113

Project Coordinator Aaron Carr
Editorial BLPS Content Connections
Designer Mandy Christiansen

Every reasonable effort has been made to trace ownership and to obtain permission to reprint copyright material. The publishers would be pleased to have any errors or omissions brought to their attention so that they may be corrected in subsequent printings.

Photo Credits
Weigl acknowledges Getty Images as as its primary photo supplier for this title. Other sources: Dreamstime: page 6 (Roman God Jupiter), NASA: page 7 (Jupiter), NASA: page 16 (Ulysses).

Contents

Introducing Jupiter 4

Naming the Planet 6

First Sightings 8

Spotting Jupiter................................ 10

Charting Our Solar System................ 12

Jupiter and Earth.............................. 14

Jupiter Today.................................... 16

Planet Watchers................................ 18

What Have You Learned? 20

Young Scientists at Work 22

Key Words/Index 23

Log on to www.av2books.com 24

Introducing Jupiter

Jupiter is the largest planet in Earth's **solar system**. It is twice the size of all the other planets combined. There are three types of planets in the solar system: rocky planets, **Gas Giants**, and **Ice Giants**. Jupiter is not made of rock like Earth. Instead, it is made up of swirling gases and forceful winds. Read on to find out more about this gigantic planet.

Jupiter looks like it has stripes. These stripes are swirling clouds.

Jupiter Facts

- It takes 12 years for Jupiter to revolve around the Sun. Earth revolves around the Sun in 365 days.

- Like Saturn, Jupiter has rings around it. Jupiter's three rings are very dark and cannot be seen with ordinary telescopes.

- The clouds around Jupiter can move at speeds of up to 400 miles (644 kilometers) per hour.

- The force of **gravity** on Jupiter is more than twice as strong as it is on Earth.

- Jupiter is called a Gas Giant. It is called a giant because it is more than 10 times the size of Earth. The other Gas Giant in the solar system is Saturn.

Naming the Planet

Ancient peoples knew about the planet Jupiter. In many different cultures, the planet was named after the king of the gods. In Roman **mythology**, Jupiter was the leader of all other gods. He was the god of light and the sky. He was also the god of **justice**.

In Greek mythology, this same god was named Zeus. The Greeks called the planet Zeus before the Romans named it Jupiter. Jupiter's moons have names from Greek mythology.

Symbols for Jupiter include the lightning bolt and the eagle.

Jupiter's Moons

Astronomers have discovered 50 moons and 16 possible moons around Jupiter. The four largest moons are Ganymede, Europa, Io, and Callisto. Ganymede is the largest moon in the solar system. Scientists believe that Europa has twice as much water as Earth. Io has active volcanoes. Callisto has many craters.

Jupiter's four largest moons were discovered in 1610.

First Sightings

Jupiter shines so brightly that people have recorded seeing it in the night sky since ancient times. After the Moon and Venus, Jupiter is the third-brightest object in the night sky.

The first person to study Jupiter was an Italian astronomer named Galileo Galilei. In 1610, he discovered Jupiter's four biggest moons. Today, the moons are called the Galilean satellites. Galileo noticed that the moons moved around Jupiter in an **orbit**. This observation proved that the planets did not orbit Earth, as people once believed.

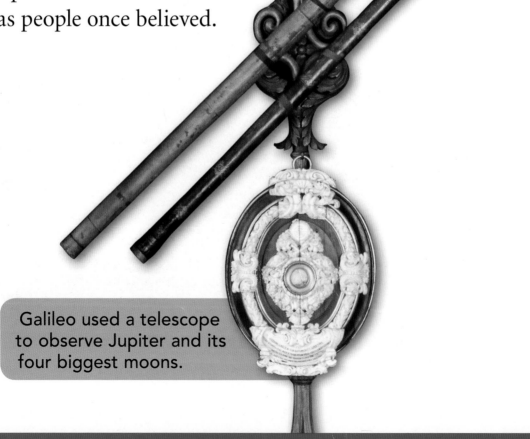

Galileo used a telescope to observe Jupiter and its four biggest moons.

Life on Jupiter?

Very little is known about Jupiter's surface. The temperature at the top of the planet's clouds is about –244° Fahrenheit (–153° Celsius). Powerful winds swirl at great speeds and blow deadly gases in all directions. People could not survive in these conditions.

Jupiter's moon Europa is like Earth in some ways. For example, Europa is thought to have an iron **core** and liquid ocean. Some scientists believe that Europa can support life.

In 2011, a team of scientists predicted that lakes of liquid water under Europa's surface may be able to support life.

Spotting Jupiter

During its orbit, Earth sometimes passes between Jupiter and the Sun. When this happens, people can see Jupiter in the night sky. Viewed through a telescope, the planet looks like a small disc. It is cream-colored and shines brightly, like a star.

Jupiter can sometimes be seen in the night sky.

See for Yourself

When viewed through binoculars, several of Jupiter's moons can be seen from Earth. They look like faint stars close to the planet. Jupiter's stripes may even be visible at times. These appear as orange, yellow, and red bands around the planet.

The Great Red Spot is a large storm that has been taking place on Jupiter for more than 300 years. The storm is a hurricane twice the size of Earth. The Great Red Spot is sometimes visible from Earth through a telescope.

Charting Our Solar System

Earth's solar system is made up of eight planets, five known dwarf planets, and many other space objects, such as **asteroids** and **comets**. Jupiter is the fifth planet from the Sun.

Sun

Mercury

Venus

Earth

Mars

Ceres

Jupiter

Order of Planets

Here is an easy way to remember the order of the planets from the Sun. Take the first letter of each planet, from Mercury to Neptune, and make it into a sentence. <u>M</u>y <u>V</u>ery <u>E</u>nthusiastic <u>M</u>other <u>J</u>ust <u>S</u>erved <u>U</u>s <u>N</u>oodles.

Eris

Makemake

Haumea

Uranus

Pluto

Neptune

Saturn

Dwarf Planets

A dwarf planet is a round object that orbits the Sun. It is larger than an asteroid or comet but smaller than a planet.

Moons are not dwarf planets because they do not orbit the Sun directly. They orbit other planets.

Jupiter and Earth

Jupiter and Earth are two very different planets. Size is the main difference. Jupiter is more than 11 times wider than Earth. In fact, Earth could be placed inside Jupiter's Great Red Spot twice and there would still be space left over. Jupiter also has 318 times more **mass** than Earth. Even though Jupiter is larger than Earth, it spins faster on its **axis**. A day on Earth is 24 hours. On Jupiter, a day is only about 10 hours.

More than 1,000 Earths could fit inside Jupiter.

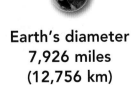

Earth's diameter
7,926 miles
(12,756 km)

Jupiter's diameter
88,732 miles
(142,800 km)

Comparing the Planets

Planets (by distance from the Sun)	Distance from the Sun	Days to orbit the Sun	Diameter	Length of Day	Mean Temperature
Mercury	36 million miles (58 million km)	88 Earth Days	3,032 miles (4,880 km)	1,408 hours	354°F (179°C)
Venus	67 million miles (108 million km)	225 Earth Days	7,521 miles (12,104 km)	5,832 hours	847°F (453°C)
Earth	93 million miles (150 million km)	365 Earth Days	7,926 miles (12,756 km)	24 hours	46°F (8°C)
Mars	142 million miles (228 million km)	687 Earth Days	4,217 miles (6,787 km)	24.6 hours	−82°F (−63°C)
Jupiter	484 million miles (778 million km)	4,333 Earth Days	88,732 miles (142,800 km)	10 hours	−244°F (−153°C)
Saturn	887 million miles (1,427 million km)	10,756 Earth Days	74,975 miles (120,660 km)	11 hours	−301°F (−185°C)
Uranus	1,784 million miles (2,871 million km)	30,687 Earth Days	31,763 miles (51,118 km)	17 hours	−353°F (−214°C)
Neptune	2,795 million miles (4,498 million km)	60,190 Earth Days	30,775 miles (49,528 km)	16 hours	−373°F (−225°C)

Jupiter Today

The first **space probe** sent to Jupiter was launched in 1972. It was called *Pioneer 10*. While traveling past Jupiter in 1973, *Pioneer 10* took many pictures and measurements of Jupiter and its moons. This information was sent back to Earth so that scientists could learn more about Jupiter.

NASA launched the space probe *Juno* in 2011. In 2016, it will enter Jupiter's orbit to study the planet more closely. *Juno* will orbit Jupiter 33 times, which will take about one year.

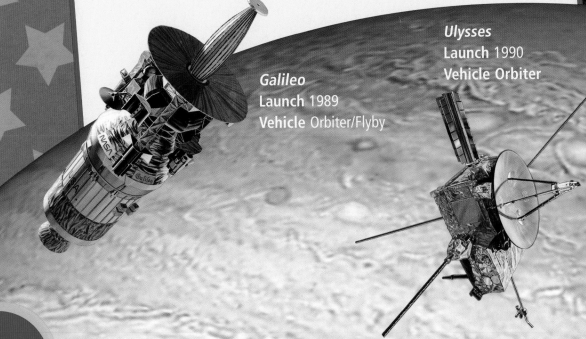

Galileo
Launch 1989
Vehicle Orbiter/Flyby

Ulysses
Launch 1990
Vehicle Orbiter

New Horizons
Launch 2006
Vehicle Flyby

Pioneer 10
Launch 1972
Vehicle Flyby

Voyager 1
Launch 2006
Vehicle Flyby

Juno
Launch 2011
Vehicle Orbiter

Cassini
Launch 1997
Vehicle Orbiter

Planet Watchers

Galileo Galilei discovered Jupiter's four main moons

Galileo Galilei is one of the most important scientists in history. He was the first person to use a telescope to look at the planets. He made his own telescope. It was much more powerful than any telescope made before. Through it, Galileo viewed the Moon and described its surface for the first time. He also risked blindness by using the telescope to look at the Sun. This was how he discovered sunspots. This telescope also helped Galileo discover Jupiter's four largest moons.

Galileo Galilei was born in Pisa, Italy, in 1564.

Scott Bolton leads NASA's Juno Mission

Scott Bolton works at NASA, where he has worked for more than 25 years. He is the principal investigator for the Juno mission to Jupiter. He also worked on two previous Jupiter missions: Cassini and Galileo.

Dr. Bolton works with a team of more than 90 scientists on the Juno mission. "Juno is a mission of discovery that could very well rewrite the books on ... how our solar system came into being," he said.

The space probe *Juno* will travel almost 1.8 billion miles (2.8 billion kilometers) during its mission.

What Have You Learned?

Take this quiz to test your knowledge of Jupiter.

1 Where does the name Jupiter come from?

2 Of the eight planets, where does Jupiter rank in size?

3 How long is a day on Jupiter?

4 What are the names of Jupiter's four biggest moons?

5 Can Jupiter be seen without a telescope?

6 What is the name of the huge storm on Jupiter?

7 Which astronomer discovered Jupiter's moons?

8 It is too cold for people to live on Jupiter. True or False?

9 How many Earth years equal one year on Jupiter?

10 Jupiter has rings around it. True or False?

Young Scientists at Work

Calculate Your Age on Jupiter

When you celebrate your birthday, you are actually celebrating one trip around the Sun. This is because we celebrate birthdays once every Earth year, or 365 days. If you lived on another planet and celebrated your birthday every time that planet went around the Sun, your age would be different.

How old would you be if you lived on Jupiter? It takes 12 Earth years for Jupiter to make one trip around the Sun. To calculate your age on Jupiter, divide your Earth age by 12.

(Your age) ÷ 12 = _____

Planets farther from the Sun take longer to orbit the Sun.

Key Words

asteroids: small, solid objects in space that circle the Sun

astronomers: people who study space and its objects

axis: an imaginary line on which a planet spins

comets: small objects in space made from dust and ice

core: the center of a planet

Gas Giants: large planets made mostly of gas; Jupiter and Saturn are the two Gas Giants in the solar system

gravity: the force that pulls objects together

Ice Giants: very cold giant planets; Neptune and Uranus are the two Ice Giants in the solar system

justice: being fair and reasonable

mass: size or bulk

mythology: stories and legends about heroes and gods

NASA: National Aeronautics and Space Administration; part of U.S. government responsible for space research

orbit: the nearly circular path a space object makes around another object in space

solar system: the Sun, the planets, and other objects that move around the Sun

space probe: a spacecraft used to gather information about space

Index

Bolton, Scott 19

Earth 4, 5, 8, 9, 10, 11, 12, 14, 15, 16
Europa 7, 9

Galilei, Galileo 8, 18, 19
Gas Giants 5
Great Red Spot 11, 14

Juno 16, 19

moons 6, 7, 8, 9, 11, 13, 16, 18
mythology 6

Pioneer 10 16, 17

space probes 16, 17
Sun 5, 10, 12, 13, 15, 18

temperature 9, 15

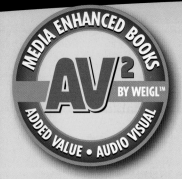

Log on to www.av2books.com

AV² by Weigl brings you media enhanced books that support active learning. Go to www.av2books.com, and enter the special code found on page 2 of this book. You will gain access to enriched and enhanced content that supplements and complements this book. Content includes video, audio, weblinks, quizzes, a slide show, and activities.

AV² Online Navigation

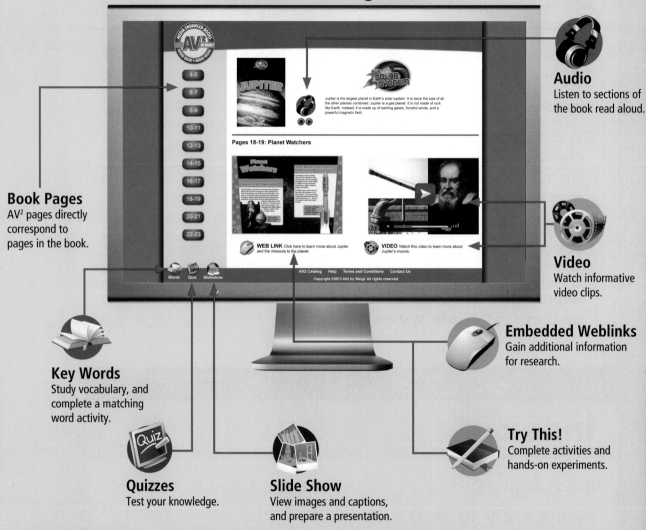

Book Pages
AV² pages directly correspond to pages in the book.

Audio
Listen to sections of the book read aloud.

Video
Watch informative video clips.

Key Words
Study vocabulary, and complete a matching word activity.

Embedded Weblinks
Gain additional information for research.

Try This!
Complete activities and hands-on experiments.

Quizzes
Test your knowledge.

Slide Show
View images and captions, and prepare a presentation.

AV² was built to bridge the gap between print and digital. We encourage you to tell us what you like and what you want to see in the future.

Sign up to be an AV² Ambassador at
www.av2books.com/ambassador.